Blueprints Science: Key Stage 2

Copymasters

BLUEPRINTS

Science
Key Stage 2
Copymasters

Second Edition

Wendy and David Clemson

Stanley Thornes (Publishers) Ltd

BLUEPRINTS – HOW TO GET MORE INFORMATION

Blueprints is an expanding series of practical teacher's ideas books and photocopiable resources for use in primary schools. Books are available for every Key Stage of every core and foundation subject, as well as for an ever widening range of other primary needs. **Blueprints** are carefully structured around the demands of National Curriculum but may be used successfully by schools and teachers not following the National Curriculum in England and Wales.

Blueprints provide:

- Total National Curriculum coverage
- Hundreds of practical ideas
- Books specifically for the Key Stage you teach
- Flexible resources for the whole school or for individual teachers
- Excellent photocopiable sheets – ideal for assessment, SATs and children's work profiles
- Supreme value.

Books may be bought by credit card over the telephone and information obtained on (0242) 228888. Alternatively, photocopy and return this FREEPOST form to join our mailing list. We will mail you regularly with information on new and existing titles.

Please add my name to the BLUEPRINTS mailing list.   *Photocopiable*

Name _____

Address_____

_____

_____

Postcode_____

To: Marketing Services Dept., Stanley Thornes Publishers, FREEPOST (GR 782), Cheltenham, Glos. GL53 1BR

First published in 1990.
Reprinted 1991.
Second Edition published in 1992 by
Stanley Thornes (Publishers) Ltd
Ellenborough House
Wellington Street
CHELTENHAM GL50 1YD

Reprinted 1993 (twice)

A catalogue record for this book is available from the British Library.

ISBN 0–7487–1494–4

Typeset by Kalligraphic Design Ltd, Horley Surrey.
Printed in Great Britain at The Bath Press, Avon.

CONTENTS

Introduction

Copymasters 1–115

Record sheets

INTRODUCTION

In this book there are 115 photocopiable copymasters linked to many of the activities in the Teacher's Resource Book. Where the copymasters are referred to in the text of the Teacher's Resource Book there are some instructions on how to use them. They are referred to by number in the Teacher's Resource Book by this symbol: ▱ . The copymasters give the children a chance to record activities and results in an organised way, and in some cases to consolidate learning that has gone before. When the children have completed these copymasters they can be added to workfiles or used as exemplar material in pupil profiles.

You may also wish to use completed copymasters as a resource for your assessments. There are two record sheets at the back of this book, on which you can note which copymasters the children have made use of, and their experience of work contributing to AT1.

At the top of each copymaster you will find symbols that explain how that sheet contributes to work on the all important Attainment Target 1: Scientific investigation. These symbols are explained in detail in the Teacher's Resource Book but they are set out here for ready reference.

Level 2

 Ask questions
 Identify
 Measure
 List
 Record findings
 Interpret findings

Level 3

 Formulate hypotheses
 Identify
 Fair/unfair test
 Use instruments
 Quantify variables
 Record
 Interpret charts
 Interpret and generalise
 Sequencing

Level 4

 Raise questions for investigation
 Formulate hypotheses
 Construct fair tests
 Identify and control variables
 Select and use instruments
 Quantify variables
 Follow instructions and diagrams
 Do it safely
 Record

 Draw tables, charts and graphs
 Draw conclusions
 Prose description

Level 5

 Investigation, selection and design
 Identify and manipulate variables
 Select and use instruments
 Quantify variables
 Statement of data patterns

Copymasters
1–115

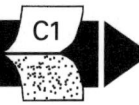

Sending messages

Join up to show where the message goes.

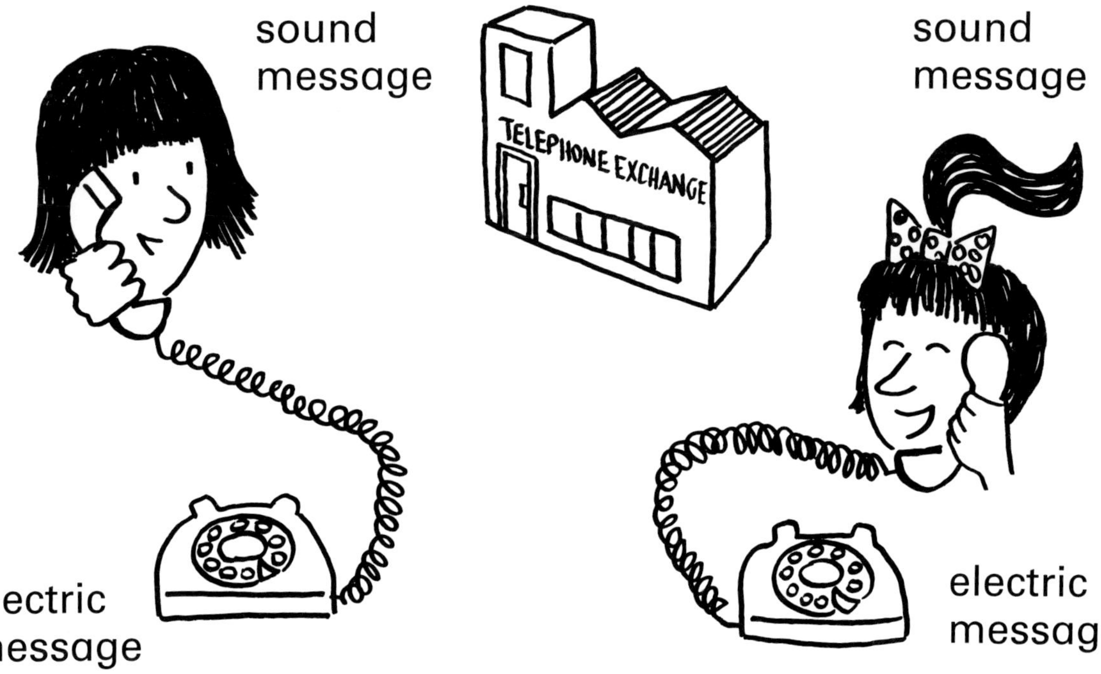

sound
message

sound
message

TELEPHONE EXCHANGE

electric
message

electric
message

Storyboard

Words	Pictures	Camera angle, etc.

Seed growing record

Pot 1	Pot 2	Pot 3	Pot 4
Growing with	Growing with	Growing with	Growing with
After 1 week	After 1 week	After 1 week	After 1 week
After 2 weeks	After 2 weeks	After 2 weeks	After 2 weeks
After 3 weeks	After 3 weeks	After 3 weeks	After 3 weeks

My needs

C4

Clothes for warmth and protection	Food and drink
Air to breathe	**Sleep**

Habits for health and safety

Clean

Well fed

Healthy and safe. That's me!

Getting enough sleep

Getting exercise

Safe on the roads

Safe at home

Two creatures compared

C6

A comparison between	
and	
Looks	
Covering	
Skeleton	
Breathing	
Food	
Sleep	
Other points	

Human and other creature compared

 C7

Me	Other creature
Covering	
Skeleton	
Breathing	
Food and drink	
Rest and sleep	
Appearance	

Differences between human beings

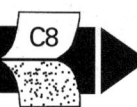

A picture of my foot beside my friend's.	Who has bigger feet?
A picture of me and . . .	Who is shorter?
A picture of my hand and my friend's hand.	Who has the longer handspan?

Contents of compost

 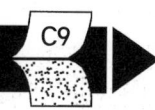

Draw things that make good compost.

Tick ✔ which make good compost.

potato peelings	grass cuttings	tins
cardboard and plastic	tea-bags	clothes

Which waste is biodegradable?

Kinds of waste we used	What we did
plastic bag can newspaper	
How long the experiment took	
The results	

Life processes 1

 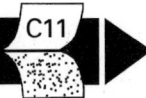
Kind of living thing		
Feeding		
Breathing		

Life processes 2

Support		
Movement		
Behaviour		

Tree reproduction

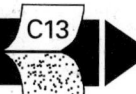 C13

This tree	Grows this fruit	Inside is this seed	Which grows into this tree
Tree →	Fruit →	Seed →	Tree
Tree →	Fruit →	Seed →	Trec

Living things reproduce their own kind  C14

Draw what the babies of these living things will grow into.

seed	tree 	seed 	
egg 	fish 	egg 	
egg 	snake 	egg 	

spawn 	tadpole 	frog 	spawn 	tadpole 	

baby rat 	adult rat 	baby rat 	
human baby 	human adult 	human baby 	

A 24-hour diary

C15

p.m.: 12, 11, 10, 9, 8, 7, 6, 5, 4, 3, 2, 1

12

a.m.: 11, 10, 9, 8, 7, 6, 5, 4, 3, 2, 1, 12

Seasonal changes and living things

 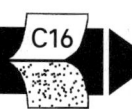
Draw and write.

| Name of living thing: |
| Season of the year: |
| Observations, e.g. appearance, growth, feeding: |

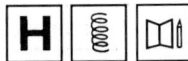
Landscape change

Our local landscape before

Our local landscape after

Waste for recycling

Kinds of reusable waste we have at home	Amount of waste produced in my family in two weeks
Newspapers 	How many?
Bottles	Green Clear Brown
Other:	

Fertilisers: for and against

Chemical fertilisers

Arguments for using them	Arguments against using them

My own views on this issue

Plants and light

Show what happens to the seedlings.

Pot 1: Full light	Pot 2: Shade	Pot 3: Darkness

Plants and water

Pot 1	Pot 2	Pot 3
Growing conditions	Growing conditions	Growing conditions
What happened	What happened	What happened

C21

Major organs

C22

Remember that the heart and urinary system go behind other organs.

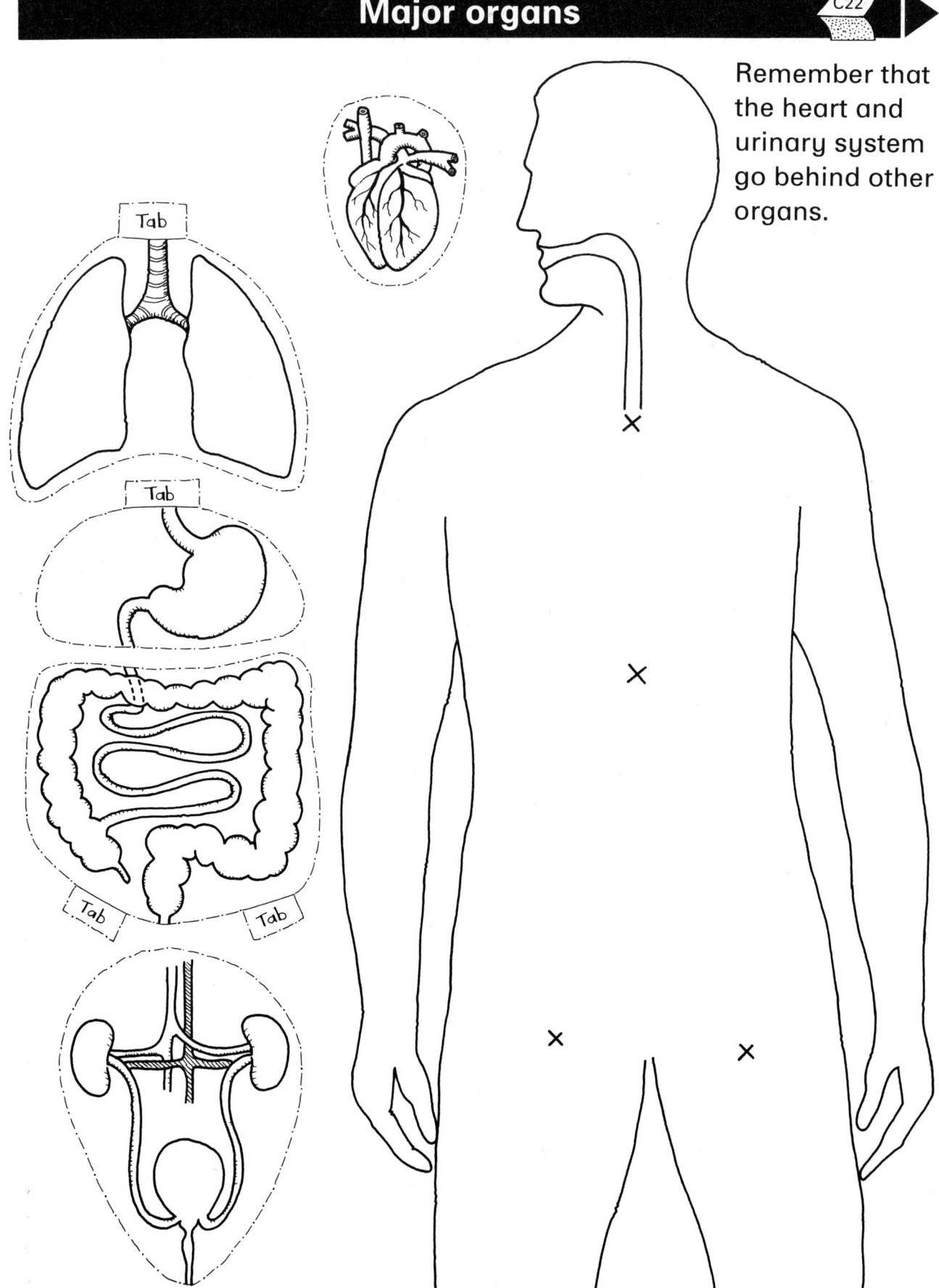

Tab

Tab

Tab

Tab

Main organs: flowering plant

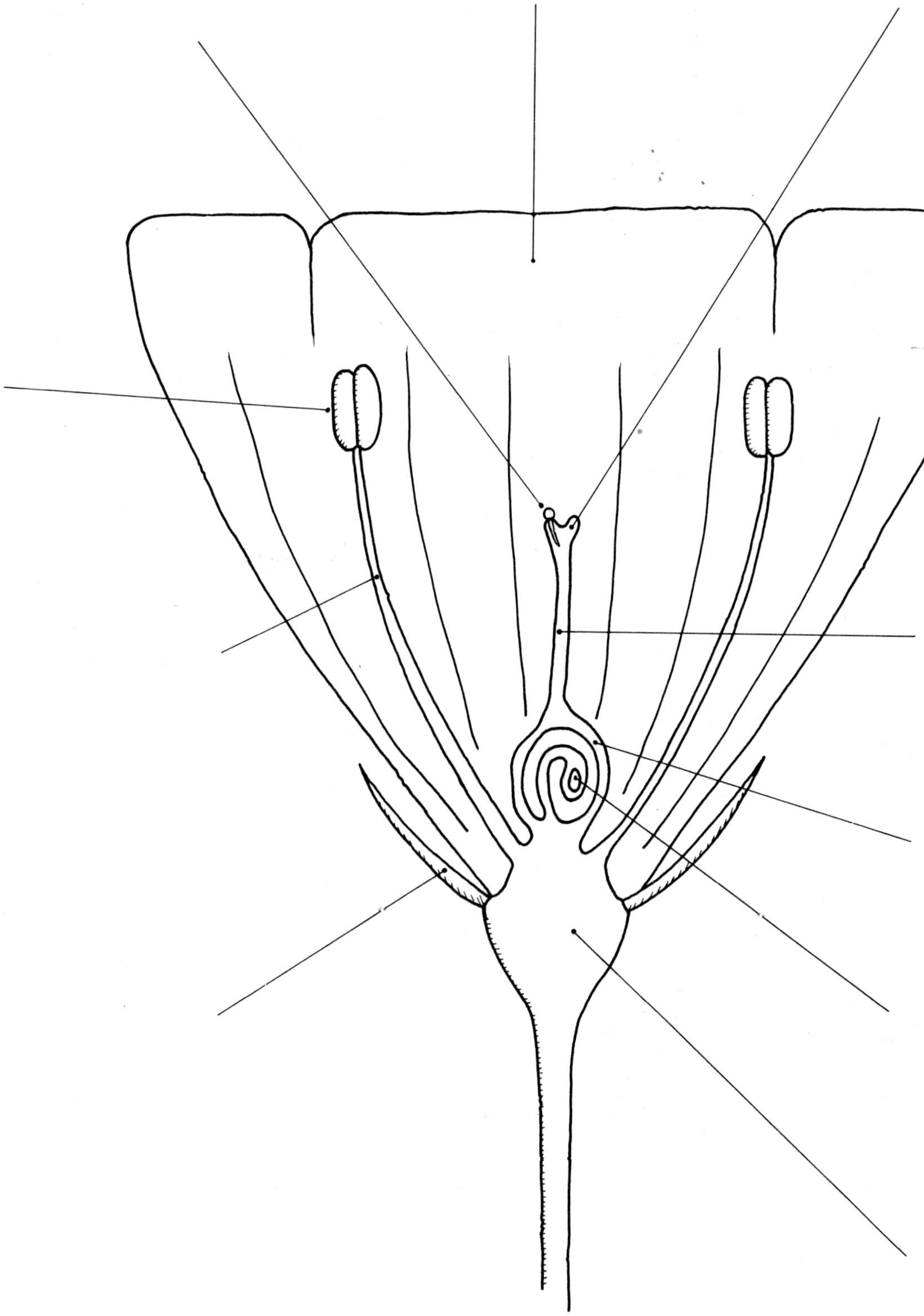

The body's defences

C24

An accident happened to me.

To make me better

These things happened inside me.	This is the help my body had.

I knew I was better when

Healthy menu

 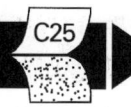

A healthy menu for a day

	Put a tick ✓ for each food eaten containing:
Breakfast	Protein
Dinner	Carbohydrate
Tea	Fats
Supper	Vitamins/minerals
Snacks	Fibre

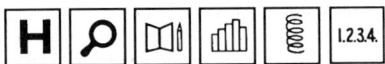

Data base record sheet

My data base is about:

Names of animals studied:

Characteristics fed into the data base:

Two things I discovered from the data base:

Some other characteristics I should like to add to my data base:

Animal variation

C27

Features to compare	Pets looked at. Draw a column for each one.		
Appearance			
Diet			
Other			

Measures of animal variation

C28

Features measured	Pets examined Draw a column for each one.	Comments on comparisons made

Comparing two localities

 C29

Draw what the _____ looks like	Draw the other
Animals or signs of animals	
Insects and other small creatures	
Birds or signs of birds	
Plants	
Other things of interest	

Temperature change

Location of thermometer

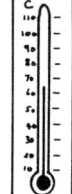

Time of observation	Temperature	Comments

C30

Action against extinction

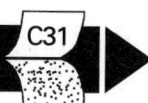

To save the   from extinction
we can act NOW. Here are some of the things people can do.

1.
2.
3.
4.
5.
6.
7.
8.
9.
10.

Fossil record

C32

Fossils from our collection	What the creatures may have looked like when alive
	$\rightarrow$
	$\rightarrow$
	$\rightarrow$

Extinct creature study

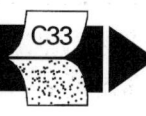

Name of extinct creature

Here is what it looked like

These are the things I found out about it

When it lived

What it ate

How it moved

Other facts about it

Organ systems: mammals

C34

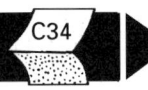

Respiratory system

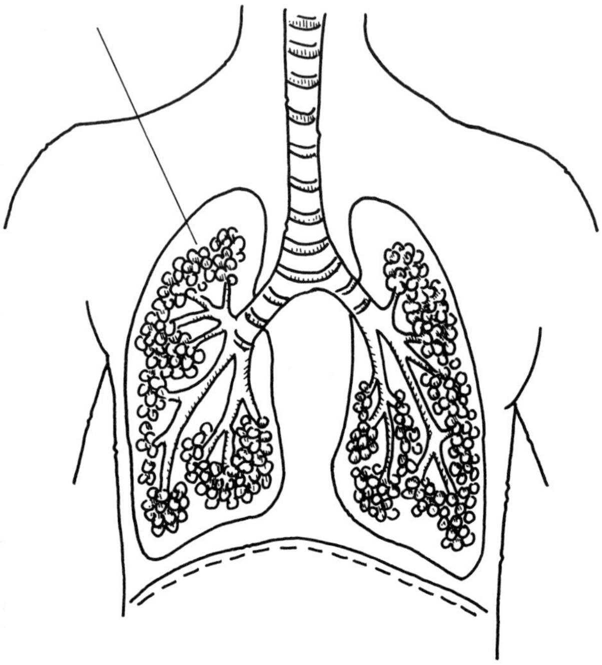

Circulatory system

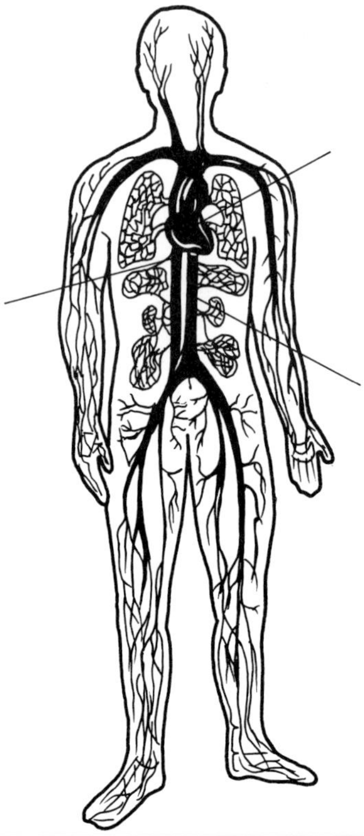

Digestive system

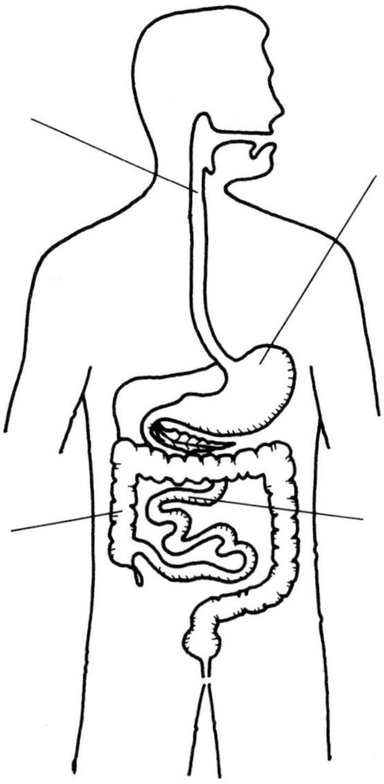

Reproductive system

Male

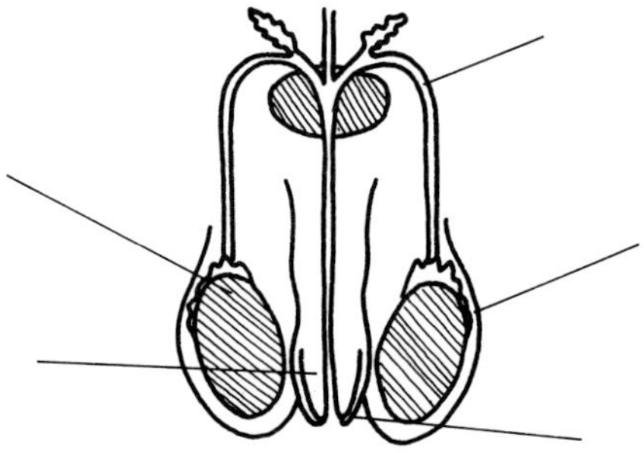

Female

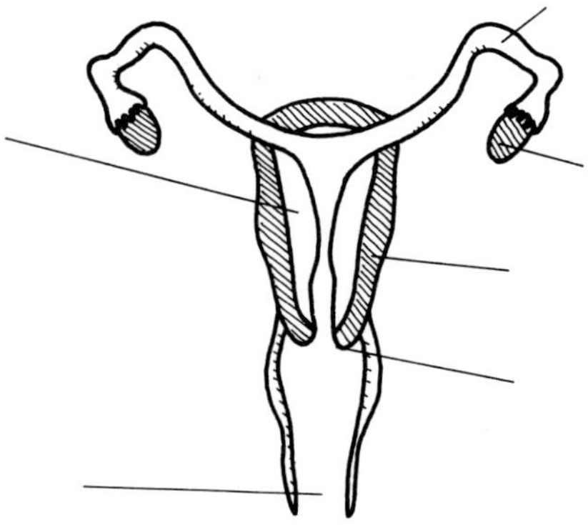

Family likeness

With the help of someone else in your family choose two people in your family whom you are said to 'take after'. Write a brief portrait of each of these people and then describe yourself, including the ways you are like these relatives.

Name Profile or full face picture	Looks Personality Habits and interests
Name Profile or full face picture	Looks Personality Habits and interests
Me Profile or full face picture	Looks Personality Habits and interests

Planning proposal role-play

C36

Name of character
Position in community
Knowledge of the plan
Concerns about the plan
Additional information learned during enquiry
Voting decision: for/against the plan

Properties of materials

Look and draw.

These are soft

These are hard

These bend and spring back

These are see-through

Ranking materials

C38

Draw each material where it comes on the scale.

Very hard   Not at all hard

Very flexible   Not at all flexible

Transparent   Not at all transparent

Heating and cooling

Draw and write.

The effect of heat on	When cooled again this is what happened.
water	
candlewax	
chocolate	
jelly	

Uses of raw materials

Draw.

Raw material	→ Use

Natural and man-made

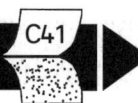

Draw and label.

In our collection these are natural materials.

These are man-made.

Raw material to raw product

Raw material	Example of the stages in between	Finished product

Weathering

Name	
What I saw  Tick ✔ and draw	Signs of weathering
Bricks	
Stone	
Tiles	
Paintwork	
Corrugated Iron	
Wood	
Other material	

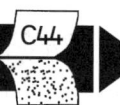

Weathering: buildings and landscape

What does the weather affect?
Write in rain/wind/sun/frost.

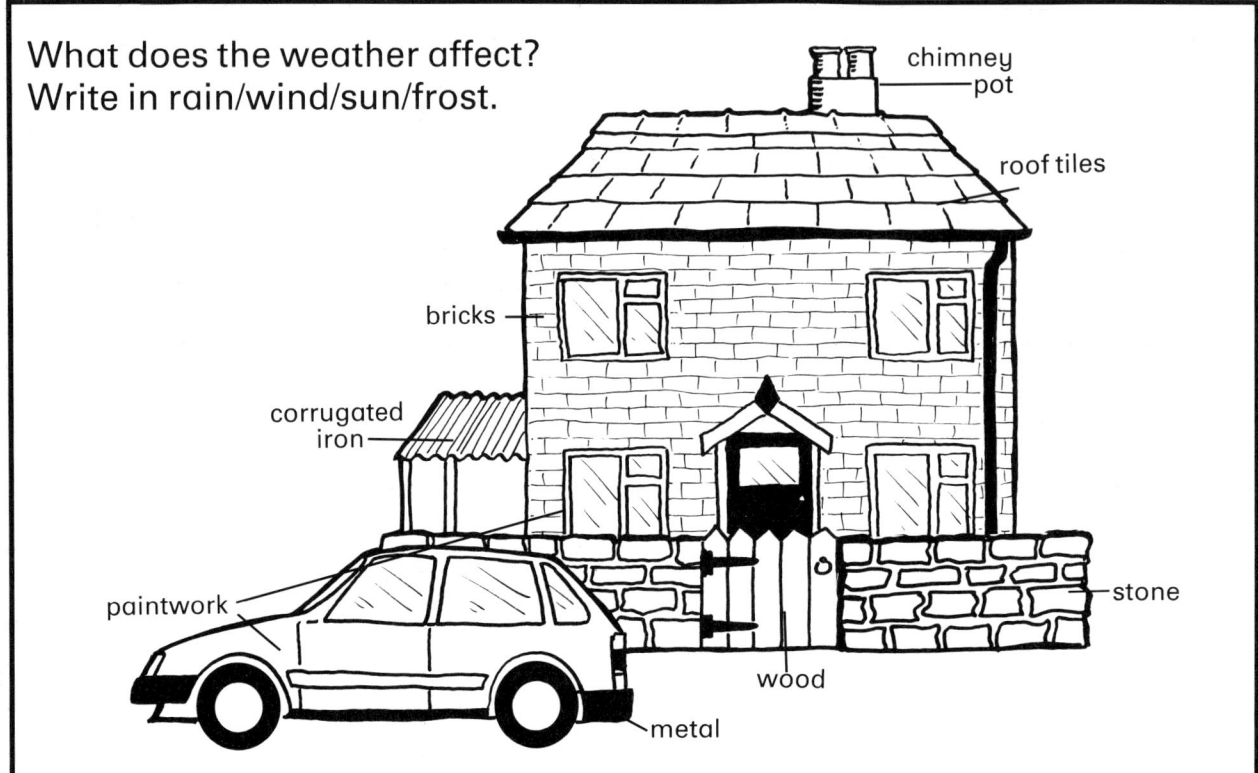

chimney pot

roof tiles

bricks

corrugated iron

stone

paintwork

wood

metal

What does the weather do to the coastline?

| High winds make the sea | What happens to the coast? |

What does the weather do to mountains?

Strength and shape in buildings

Tick the 'strong' shapes. How do you know they are strong?

Draw some common shapes you spotted in building construction.

Tick the 'strong' shapes. How do you know they are 'strong'?

Concrete in buildings is often in square and rectangular shapes.
How is the concrete in these shapes made stronger?

Hardness of materials

Draw and name the hardest material you tested.

Draw the other materials in order of hardest to softest, starting with the hardest.

Use of materials

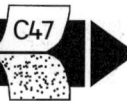

C47

Draw and label your inventions to show what they are made of.	Reasons for your choice of materials.

Solubility at different temperatures

C48

Solution	Cold water		Warm water		Hot water	
	Temperature of water	Time taken to dissolve (secs)	Temperature of water	Time taken to dissolve (secs)	Temperature of water	Time taken to dissolve (secs)

Solids, liquids, gases

C49

	Examples	Their uses
Solids		
Liquids		
Gases		

Weather record

Monday	Tuesday	Wednesday	Thursday	Friday

Weather report/forecast

Group

Weather report/forecast for   (date)

The weather is:

Here is a map of our part of the country showing the weather today:

The forecast is:

Weather summary:

Measuring temperature

C52

Temperature chart	Dates:			
Day	Inside our classroom	Outside in the playground	Temperature in the forecast	Who wrote on this chart
Mon				
Tues				
Wed				
Thurs				
Fri				

Mon				
Tues				
Wed				
Thurs				
Fri				

Mon				
Tues				
Wed				
Thurs				
Fri				

Rainfall recording

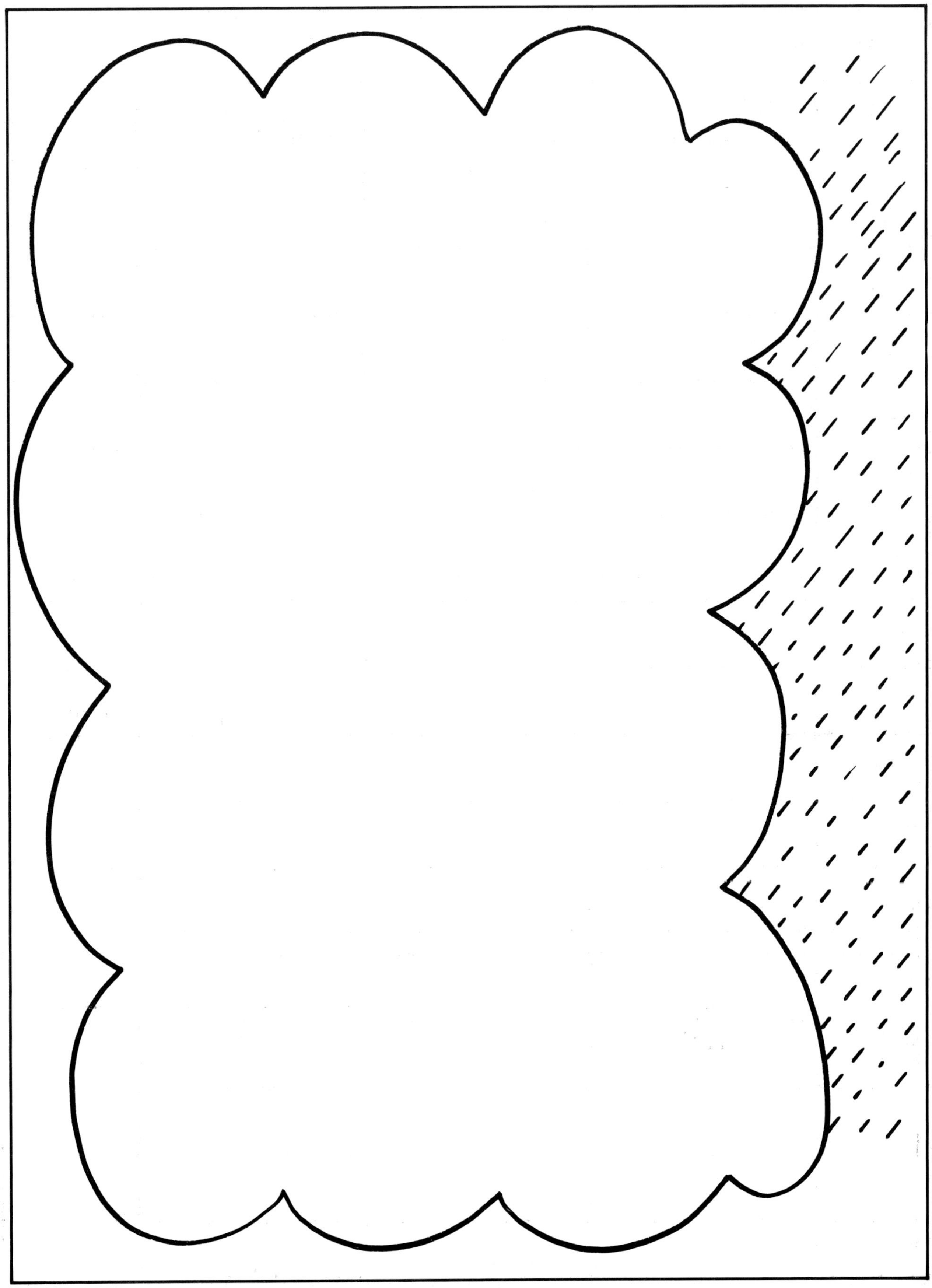

Measuring wind speed/direction 1

Our invention shows

It is called a

Our names

This is how we made it

This is how it works

Measuring wind speed/direction 2

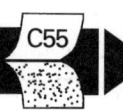

C55

The Magnificent New

Flying a kite?   Sailing a boat?   Doing the washing?

Get wind-wise with

Made only of

This is the fantastic job it does

Recommended by

Rock and soil investigation

Kind of rock

Colours

How it looks

How it feels

Does it weather easily?

Under the magnifier it looks

Soil
Colours

How it feels

Weigh how much fills a small flowerpot   g.
Do you think it is fertile?
Why do you think that?

Plant a seed in the soil.
Did it germinate?
How many days did it take to germinate?

Effects of water, wind and ice

Write a report suitable for a magazine, about the effects of water, wind and ice on the landscape. Create a headline, include the main facts in order and give some real locations as examples.

Water

Wind

Ice

Classifying solutions

Solution	Result of litmus test	Results of universal indicator test

The water cycle

The water cycle

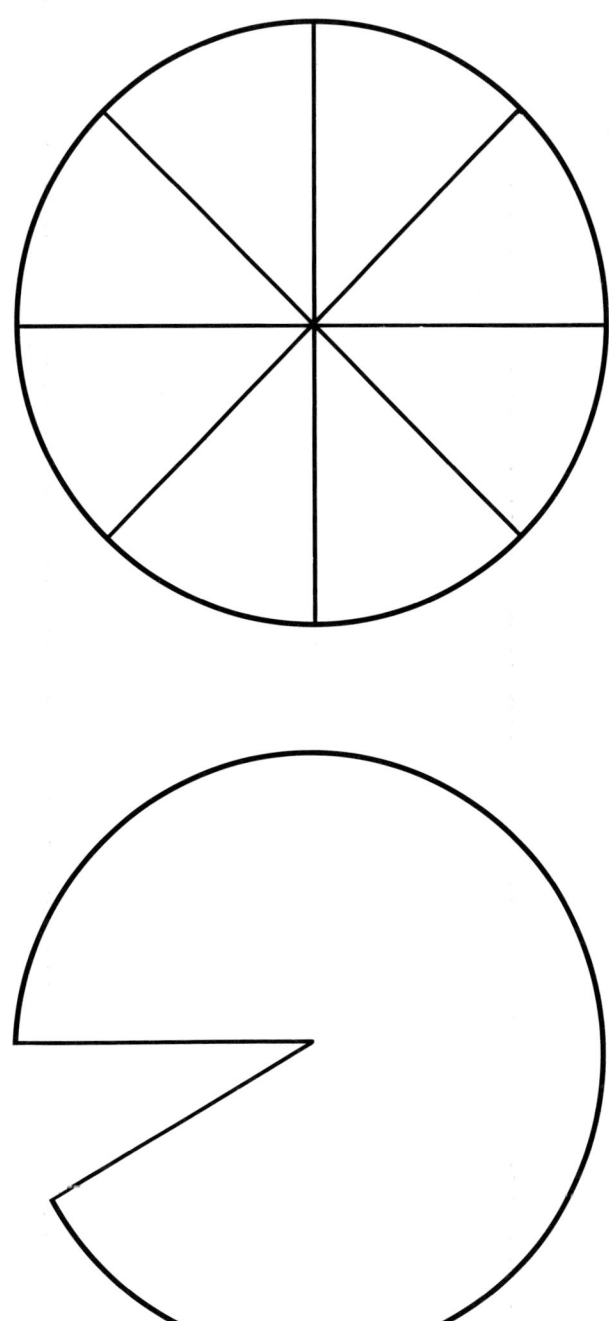

1. Cut out two circles of card. The larger one needs to be at least 16 cm across, the other slightly smaller.
2. Find the centre of the larger circle, and then mark in eight sectors of equal size.
3. Write in one step of the water cycle on each sector, following in order round your circle.
4. The smaller circle then has ⅛th sector cut out. Fix this circle over the larger one with a paper fastener pushed through the centres.

What is attracted by a magnet?

Tick ✓ the things attracted by a magnet.

Draw some more things in the empty boxes.

drawing pin	pin	pencil	metal pipe	paper	pottery cup
cardboard	wood	chalk	plastic	metal scissors	2p coin
cork	candle	marble	paper fastener	clothes peg	plastic button
steel wool	cotton wool	brass button	10p coin	rubber	glass
Sellotape	clay	wax crayon	rubber band	sea shell	bolt
pebble	rubber ball	ribbon	leaf	stick	shoe buckle
gold ear-ring	Lego	gold ring	coat hook	PE shoe	drinks can
bottle top	plastic comb	matchbox			

Which way is north?

Draw a picture of the classroom as seen from the ceiling (fly's view). Lay the drawing on your desk so that it is facing the same way as the room.

Put a compass on your picture. Mark N where the needle stops. Take away the compass. Draw an arrow pointing North.

Hot and cold

Me in winter clothes:

Me in summer clothes:

Heat insulation

Draw the bottles.
Name the materials.

Draw the bottles.

Stayed
warmest

Cooled
quickest

Measuring air temperature

How I set up the experiment

Temperature readings

How I explain my results

Temperature of a liquid

Hot drink used		
Shapes of cup	Temperature readings	Temperature drop during experiment

Shape which keeps drink hottest

Push and pull in sport

Tick ✓ push and/or pull.
Talk to your teacher about your work.

Skate	Skateboard	Football: kick!
push pull	push pull	push pull
Table tennis: hit!	Tug of war	Rounders: hit!
push pull	push pull	push pull
Swimming	Cycling	Bowling
push pull	push pull	push pull

C66

Push and pull with hand tools

C67

Tick ✓ push and/or pull.
Talk to your teacher about your work.

hammer	saw	chisel
push pull	push pull	push pull
plane	sandpaper	pulley
push pull	push pull	push pull

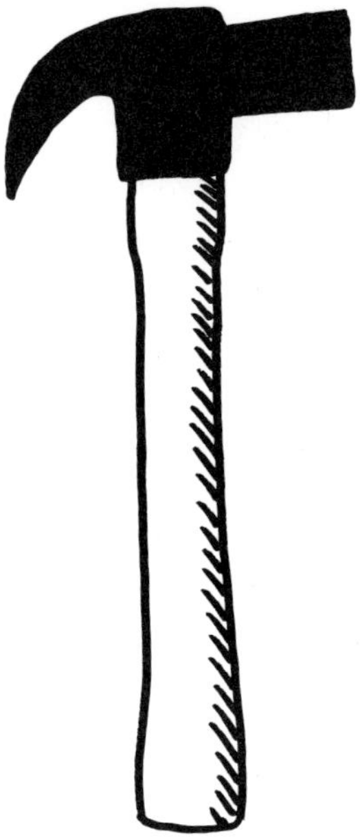

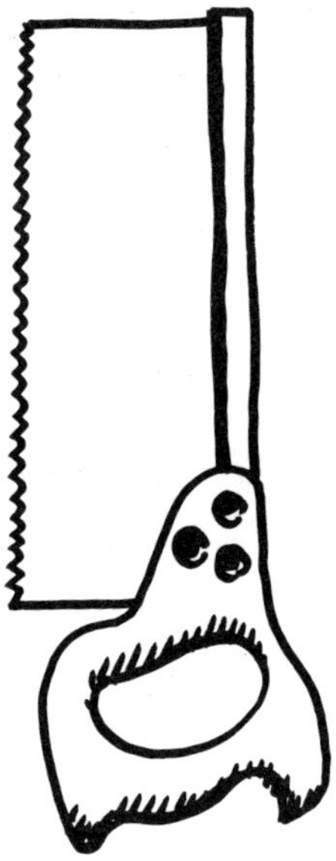

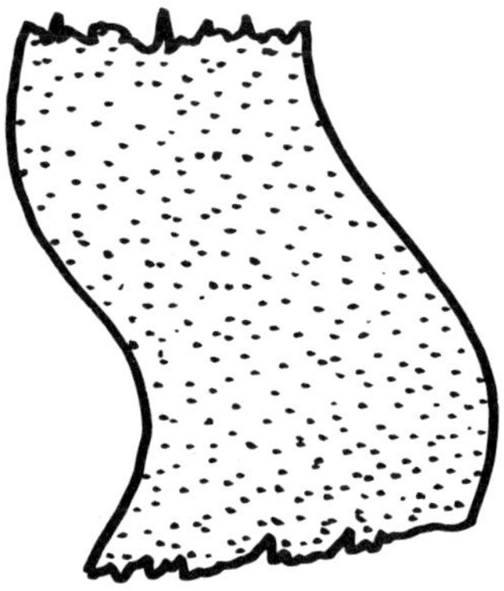

Shadow puppets

My puppet is called:

How I made my puppet:

What my puppet looks like:

How to work my puppet:

Earth, Sun and Moon

Earth facts

Sun facts

Moon facts

Electrical safety at home

C70

Draw 4 electrical hazards in your home.

Electrical circuits

Complete the circuits.

What happens?

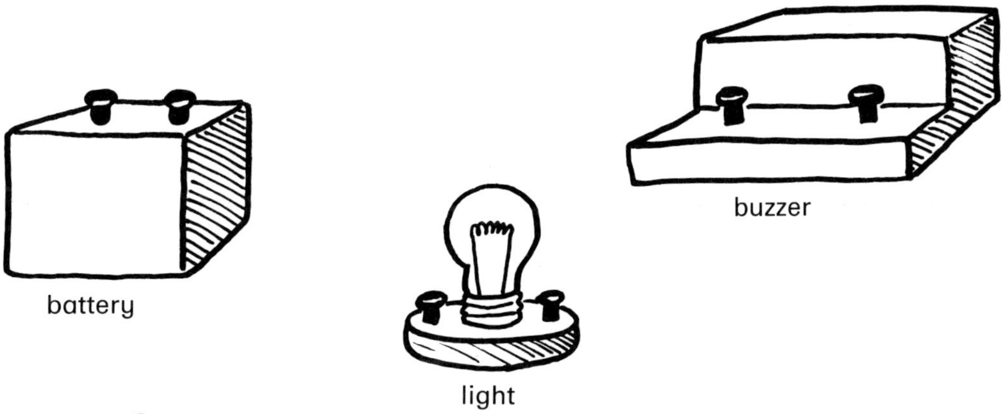

What happens?

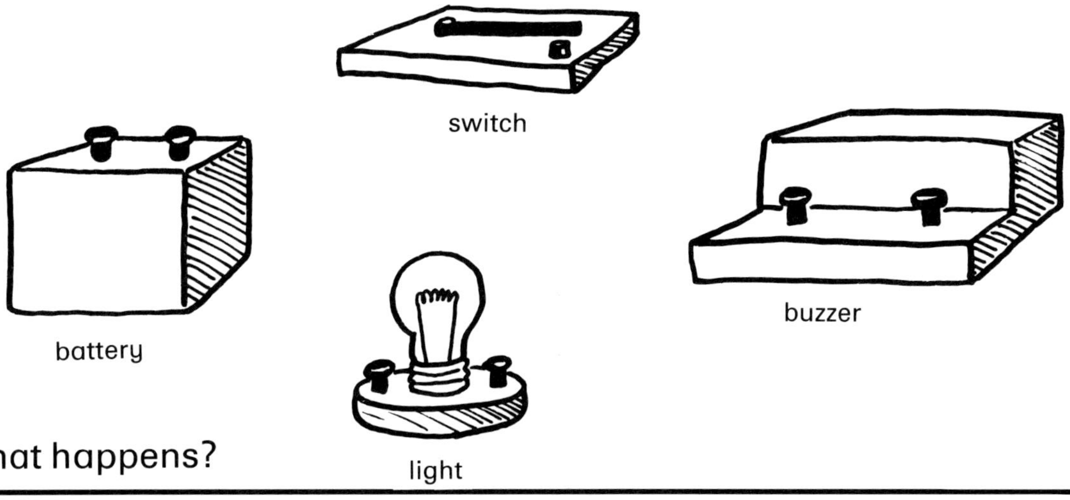

What happens?

Good and bad conductors

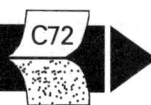 C72

Draw your circuit here.

What was added to complete the circuit?	What happened?	Is it a good or bad conductor?

Start and stop force

Two ways I found to start the car. Draw and write.

1.

2.

What made the car start?

1.   2.

Two ways I found to stop the car. Draw and write.

1.

2.

What made the car stop?

1.   2.

Paper aeroplane

 C74

Take a rectangle of paper.

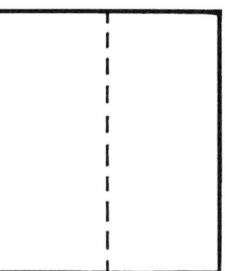

1. Make a fold down centre and open out.

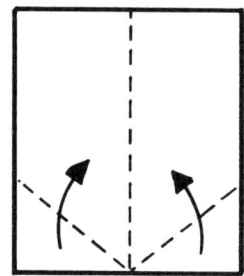

2. Fold 2 corners up to centre line.

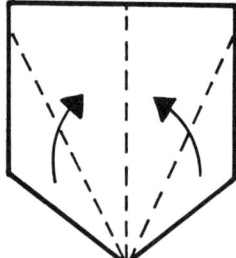

3. Fold 2 corners up to centre fold.

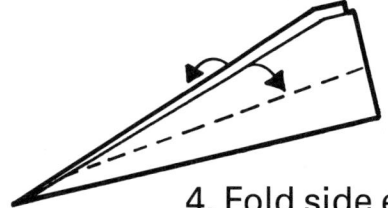

4. Fold side edges down to centre fold on outside.

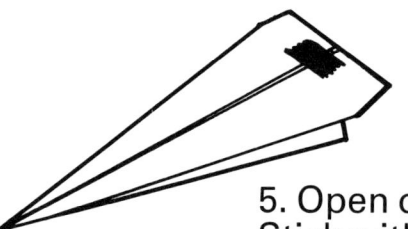

5. Open out. Stick with tape.

Draw a new design here.

Make it and see if it flies better than the other model.

Reflections

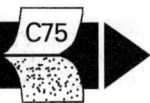

Make a list of 10 things in which you can see your reflection.

Sometimes your reflection looks unlike the 'real' you. Draw the real you and two funny reflections you have seen.

The real me	Funny 1	Funny 2

Moon phases

Record the date and the Moon's shape once each week.

Date Shape of Moon	Date Shape of Moon
Date Shape of Moon	Date Shape of Moon

Me and my shadow

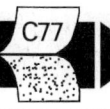

C77

Work out a scale for your drawing and write in the scale.

This is me	This is my summer shadow at a.m./p.m.	This is my winter shadow at a.m./p.m.
↓	↓	↓

Tick ✓ what is true.

Summer	Sun	higher/lower in sky
	shadows	longer/shorter
Winter	Sun	higher/lower in sky
	shadows	longer/shorter

Electrical circuits in models

Draw your circuit.

Describe how you made the circuit.

Draw what the circuit does for your final model.

Morse

Draw your Morse circuit.

Write your message in longhand

and in Morse

Now write the reply in longhand

and in Morse

What makes toys go?

Draw some toys.	Is the energy stored?	What makes them go?
'push' toys		
clockwork toys		
flywheel toys		
battery toys		
mains electricity toys		

What makes machines go?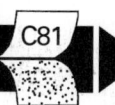

Machine	What makes it go?
washing machine	
calculator	
computer	
clock	
lamp	
torch	
pencil sharpener	

Energy stores

Name and draw some things in which energy is stored.	In what form is the energy released?

Gravitational force

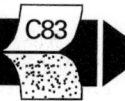 C83

Where we did the experiment		
Timing devices used		
What was dropped	**What happened**	**Comments**

Pendula investigation

 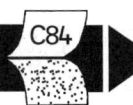

What did not change during this experiment
(length, weight or starting arc)?

What were the variables?

How the experiment was set up

Results (Put them in a table.)

Floating and sinking

What is it? Draw or write.	What happened?	
	Floated	Sank

Friction investigation

Kind of surface under block	Number of masses or blocks which start it moving

Comments on results

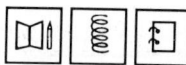

Sound takes time

The experiment was to find out

This is what we did (words or pictures)

This is what happened (words or pictures)

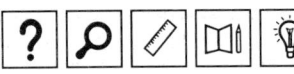

Day length study

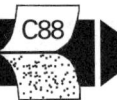

Colour day yellow and night blue.

Date	a.m.												p.m.											
	1	2	3	4	5	6	7	8	9	10	11	12	1	2	3	4	5	6	7	8	9	10	11	12

Measuring time using the Sun

C89

9 a.m.	10 a.m.	11 a.m.	12 noon	1 p.m.	2 p.m.	3 p.m.	4 p.m.

Draw in skyline.
Stick on red summer Suns or yellow winter Suns.

Sundials

My sundial

Other kinds of sundials

Telling the time without a clock

On   (date) I estimated the time
was
These are the clues I found to tell the time.

On my sundial the time was   a.m./p.m.
My sundial looked like this.

My teacher said the time on the clock
was   a.m./p.m.

My estimation was close to the correct time/not close enough!

Time around the world

The date today
Our time:

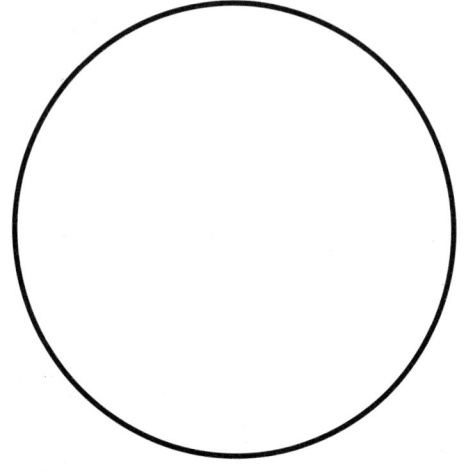

The time in . . .
is . . .

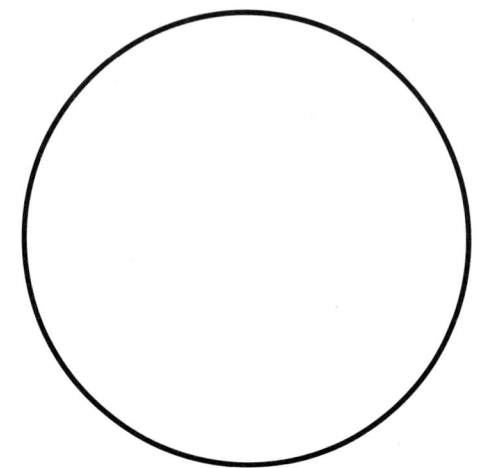

The time in . . .
is . . .

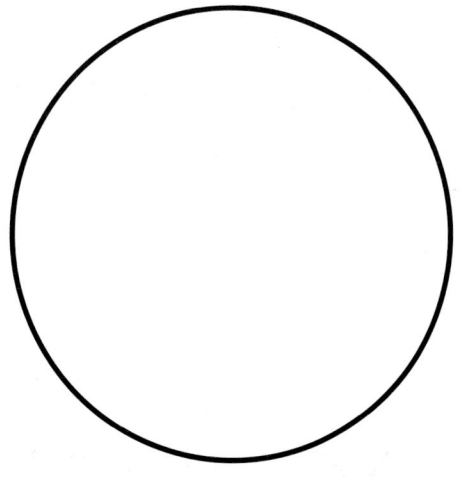

The time in . . .
is . . .

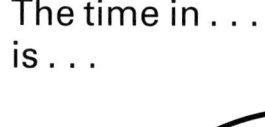

Comments

Circuit symbols

Cell	Lamp	Switch

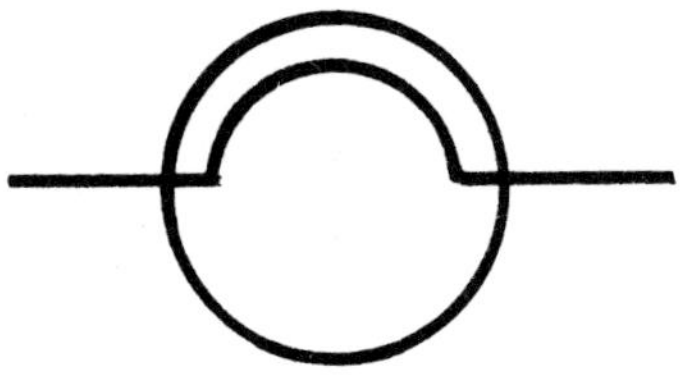

Wires joined	Wires crossed	Fuse

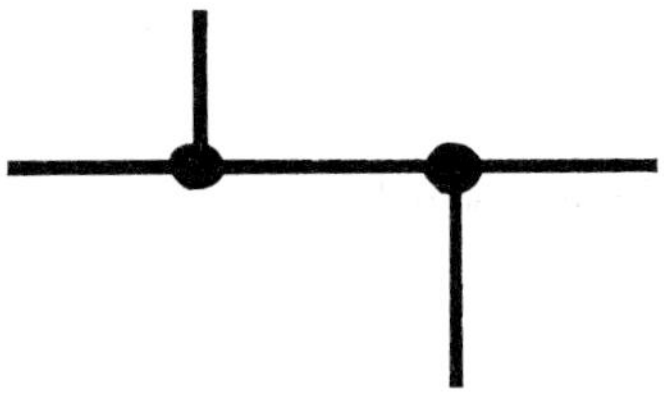

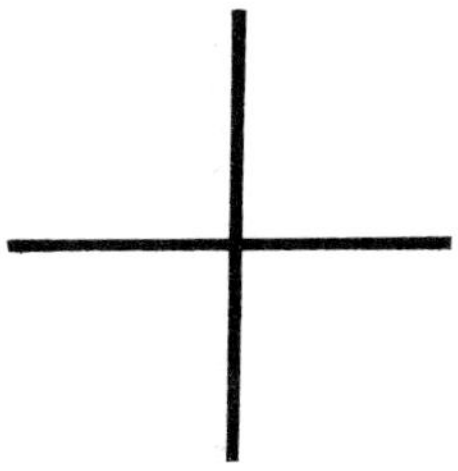

Ammeter	Voltmeter

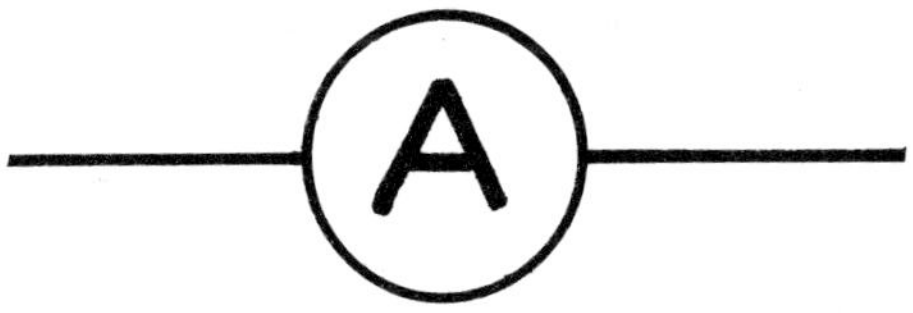

Fixed resistor	Variable resistor

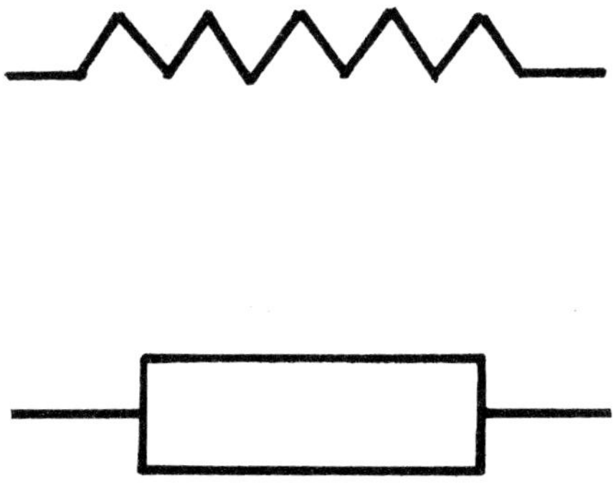

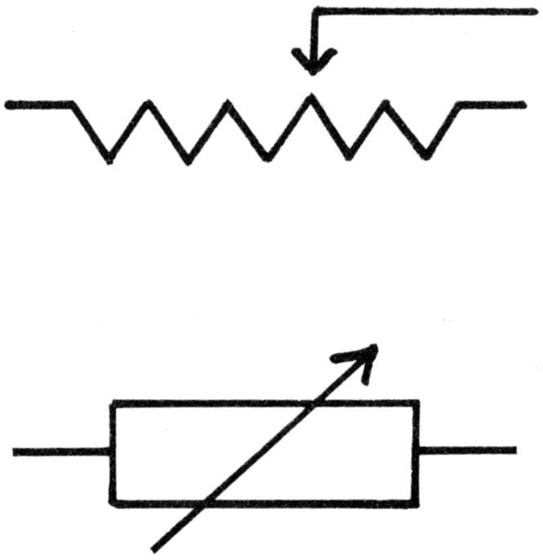

Circuit experiments

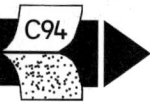

Draw some of the circuits you have made.

Series circuits

Parallel circuits

Resistance: railway controller

Position of indicator on controller	Time taken for train to go round 10 times (seconds)	Comments on results

Effect of variable resistor

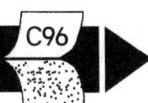

The circuit

Draw resistor and indicate position of control	Brightness of bulb 1 = dim 5 = dazzling	Comments

Switches

C97

Switches I invented:

Switch 1 goes on or off when released

✓ or ✗

Easy to use ☐   Durable ☐
Easy to connect ☐   Well constructed ☐

Switch 2 slides on or off and remains so

✓ or ✗

Easy to use ☐   Durable ☐
Easy to connect ☐   Well constructed ☐

Thermostats at home

Name of appliance	Description of thermostat. Where is it? Can you see it/its control? How does the control look?	Temperature range used by appliance (if known)

Logic gates game

C99

START 1	2	GATE 3	4	5	6	7	8	9	10	11	GATE 12
24	23	22	GATE 21	20	19	18	17	16	GATE 15	14	13
25	GATE 26	27	28	29	30	GATE 31	32	33	34	35	36
FINISH 48	47	46	45	GATE 44	43	42	41	40	39	GATE 38	37

4 OR 5	6 OR 1	2 OR 3	AND
AND	NOT 6	NOT 5	NOT 3
		AND	NOT 1

Cut out these small cards. Shuffle them and put them in a pile face down. Play the game with a friend. Throw a die and move your counter. When you land on a GATE square take a card from the pile. If AND throw die twice at next turn and move the sum of throw 1 AND 2. If OR you must throw one of these numbers to move next go. If NOT, then you need any other number than that to move.

You need:
1 die
2 counters
2 players

Energy use

Tick ✓ which takes more energy.
Does it take more energy
to   or

eat an apple   run a mile?

lie in bed   climb a ladder?

jump a fence   look at a book?

play tiddly-winks   play golf?

swim a length   have a nap?

walk to school   run to school?

clean the car   watch television?

go round the supermarket   write a shopping list?

Is energy essential?

What are the things we could do without? Are there things we would not be able to do? What might we use instead?
If there was no

Electricity

Coal

Oil

Paddle-boat

How I made my paddle-boat

Results of 'test' sailings

How I could improve the design

Windmill

You need   paper or thin card
strip of thick card
pencil
ruler
scissors
paper fastener

Cut out an exact square of paper with sides of 15 cm. Fold along the diagonals.

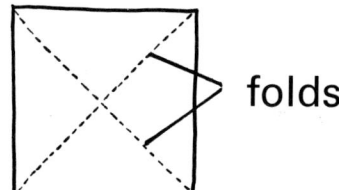 folds

Make 8 cm cuts along the diagonals towards the centre.

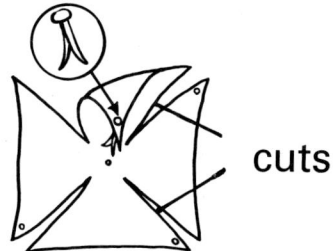 cuts

Take corners into centre and attach a paper fastener through all layers of paper and through one end of the card strip.

Your windmill is ready.

Speed and stopping distance

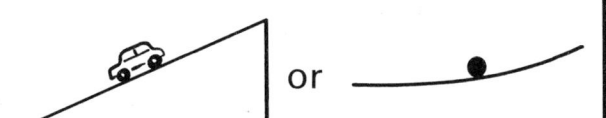

Trial number	Distance travelled (cm)

Average distance travelled (cm)	

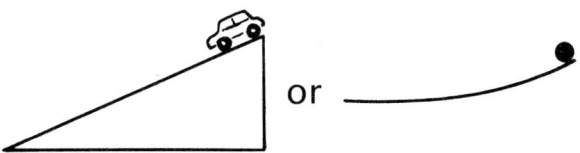

Trial number	Distance travelled (cm)

Average distance travelled (cm)	

Conclusions	

Stopping force

C105

Name or number of vehicle	Distance pump cylinder pushed	Comments

? 🔍 ⏱ 🥤 🅰🅱

Stretching spring

Starting length (cm)	Masses added (g)	Stretched length (cm)	Amount of 'stretch'	Comments

Put your results on a graph with axes like this:

masses
added
(g)

length (cm)

Distance/time experiment

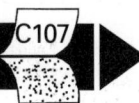

Trial No.	Outward distance travelled (m/cm)	Trial No.	Return distance travelled (m/cm)
Average distance travelled		Average distance travelled	

Put your results on a graph with axes like this:

distance (m)

time (seconds)

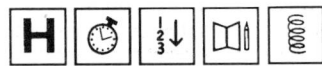

Reflection

Put your mirror on this line.
Direct the light beam at the mirror. Draw in the
route the beam takes to the mirror and after it
has touched the mirror. Move the light beam and
draw its route again. Do this several times.

What do you notice?

Single mirror investigation

Use a mirror to help you finish the pictures.

How many ways can you place the mirror so that only two buttons are reflected?

Write about a discovery you have made about mirrors.

Instruments

Draw

Instruments we blow phoo!	Instruments we pluck ping!

Instruments we bang boom!

Vibration experiment

Draw the sand on the drum before the experiment.

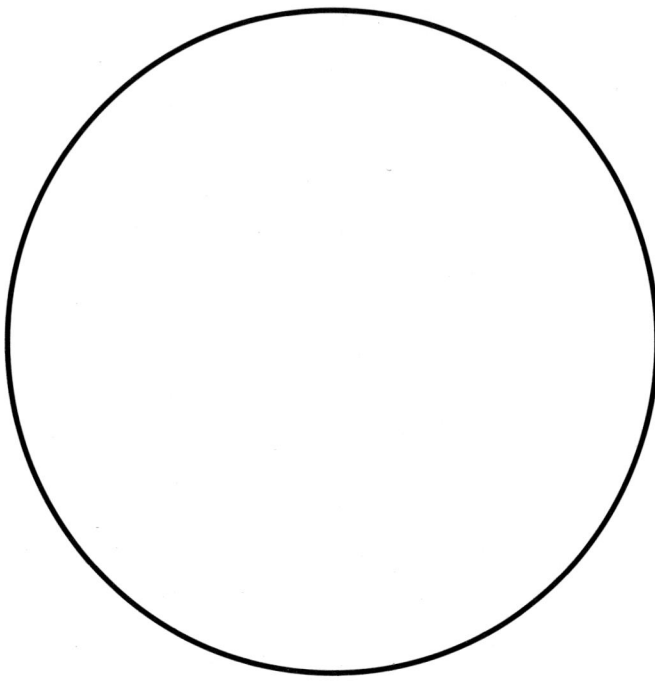

Draw the sand on the drum after the tuning fork has been put on it.

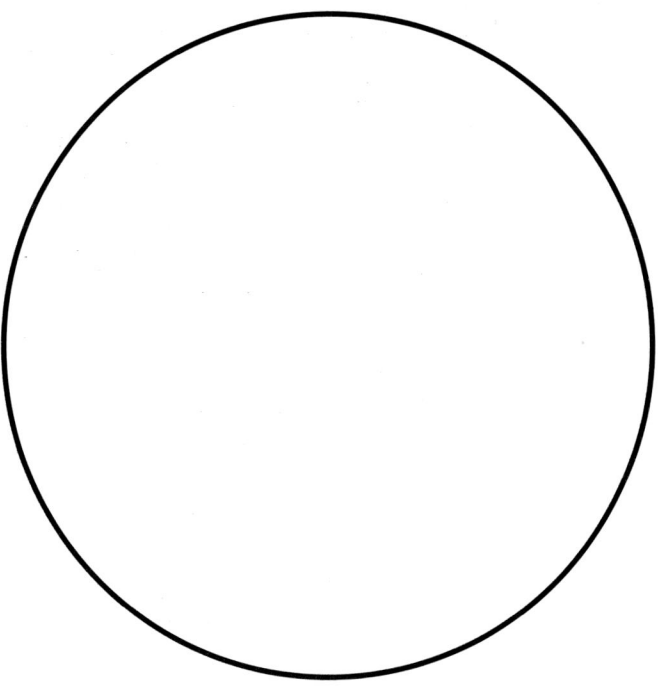

Annoying noise

blah! blah!

bbrrrring!

scritch!

clink!

yeeowl!

plop

poof!

rustle

aargh!

tick tock!

bang!

click click!

boom!

Noise investigation

C113

Investigation details

Where the recordings were made

When the recordings were made

Comments about the investigation

Star facts

1. The most important thing I learned is:

2.

My six discoveries about stars

3.

4.

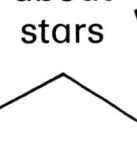

5.

6.

My stars

My star sign is

and the constellation looks like this

It is called

My birthday is

Name _____ Year/Class _____

Level 2	?							▦											
	🔍							📖✏											
	📏							💡											
Level 3	**H**							📖✏											
	🔍							▮▮											
	⚖							🌀											
	⏱							1.2.3.4.											
	🫗																		
Level 4	?							1 2 3 ↓											
	H							✓											
	⚖							📖✏											
	🔍							📈											
	⏱							🌀											
	🫗							🗒											
Level 5	?							🫗											
	🔍							A B											
	⏱																		

Key Stage Two

Name

Year/Class

	Level 2			Level 3			Level 4			Level 5		
	Comments			Comments			Comments			Comments		
AT 2	a	b	c	a	b	c	a	b	c	a	b	c
AT 3	a	b	c	a	b	c	a	b	c	a	b	c
AT 4	a	b	c	a	b	c	a	b	c	a	b	c